If you're a chicken lover looking for easy and fast recipes that the whole family can enjoy, then this book is perfect for you. It contains delicious chicken recipes that are healthy and easy to make. From classic dishes like roasted chicken and chicken soup to creative options like chicken tacos and wings, there's something for everyone in this book. All the recipes are easy to follow with easy-to-find ingredients, and most can be prepared in under 30 minutes. With this book, you can learn how to make delicious chicken meals that everyone in your family will love! Enjoy easy and healthy meals with this chicken recipes book. It's the perfect cookbook for busy families who want to eat delicious food without spending a lot of time in the kitchen. You'll be able to make amazing dishes that are sure to please everyone at the table!

Italian Chicken Skillet

Looking for delicious chicken recipes that are easy and fast to make? Look no further! This delicious Italian Chicken Skillet with Sun-Dried Tomatoes is the perfect dish for busy weeknights. Made with delicious seasonings like rosemary, garlic, onion, sun dried tomatoes and spinach this one-pan meal will be a hit in your household. Plus, you can make it dairy-free by swapping out the heavy cream for a can of coconut cream or homemade cashew cream and topping with nutritional yeast instead of cheese. Ready in under 30 minutes, this delicious Italian Chicken Skillet with Sun Dried Tomatoes will become a regular at your dinner table! Enjoy!

This delicious Italian Chicken Skillet with Sun-Dried Tomatoes is the perfect weeknight dinner! With delicious seasonings like rosemary, garlic, onion, sun dried tomatoes and spinach this easy one-pan meal comes together in under 30 minutes. Make it dairy-free by swapping out the heavy cream for a can of coconut cream or homemade cashew cream and topping with nutritional yeast instead of cheese. Enjoy this delicious chicken dish that is easy, fast and delicious!

Make delicious Italian Chicken Skillet with Sun-Dried Tomatoes in no time! This delicious one-pan meal combines rosemary, garlic, onion, sun dried tomatoes and spinach for a flavorful dinner the whole family will love. Make it dairy-free by swapping out the heavy cream for a can of coconut cream or homemade cashew cream and topping with nutritional yeast instead of cheese. Ready in under 30 minutes, this delicious Italian Chicken Skillet with Sun Dried Tomatoes will become a regular at your dinner table! Enjoy!

Chicken Fried Rice

Chicken Fried Rice is a delicious, easy and fast meal that you can prepare in minutes. It's one of the most popular chicken recipes around, and it's easy to see why! This comfort food dish packs plenty of flavor and nutrition all into one easy-to-make meal.

The ingredients in Chicken Fried Rice are simple, but the flavors are anything but. Start by heating oil (both sesame and vegetable) in a wok or large skillet over medium-high heat. Once hot, add chicken breasts and sauté until cooked through. Add frozen peas and carrots, green onions, garlic, eggs and cooked rice to the pan and cook until everything is heated through. Finally, stir in low-sodium soy sauce for some added flavor and serve.

With just a few simple ingredients and easy steps, you can have a delicious meal ready to go in no time! So next time you're looking for an easy and flavorful chicken recipe, give Chicken Fried Rice a try - it's sure to be a hit!

Happy cooking!

Chicken Pot Pie

INGREDIENTS

1 POUND SKINLESS, BONELESS CHICKEN BREAST HALVES - CUBED.
1 CUP SLICED CARROTS.
1 CUP FROZEN GREEN PEAS.
½ CUP SLICED CELERY.
⅓ CUP BUTTER.
⅓ CUP CHOPPED ONION.
⅓ CUP ALL-PURPOSE FLOUR.
½ TEASPOON SALT. GREAT VALUE IODIZED SALT, 26 OZ.

Chicken pot pie is an easy and fast recipe that is perfect for busy weeknights. It's a comforting dish filled with cubed chicken, carrots, peas, celery, butter, onion and all-purpose flour that can be prepared in no time. To make this easy chicken recipe even tastier, you can add ½ teaspoon of salt for seasoning.

If you are looking for easy and fast chicken recipes, then this is the one for you. All you have to do is cube the chicken breasts, slice the carrots and celery, gather all other ingredients and mix them together in a large bowl until everything is well combined. Then transfer the mixture into an oven-safe dish and bake for about 30 minutes or until golden brown. Enjoy your easy and delicious chicken pot pie!

That's all there is to making this easy chicken pot pie recipe. With just a few easy steps, you can prepare a comforting and delicious meal in no time. So if you're looking for easy and fast chicken recipes to make for dinner, then this easy chicken pot pie should be your go-to dish.

The key to making the perfect chicken pot pie is to use all the ingredients listed above and season it with Great Value Iodized Salt for added flavor. With just a few easy steps, you can have a delicious meal that's ready in no time! So, next time you're looking for easy and fast chicken recipes, give this easy chicken pot pie a try. Enjoy!

Chicken Cacciatore

Chicken Cacciatore is an easy and fast chicken recipe that can be prepared in no time. It's a hearty yet healthy Italian dish made with bone-in, skin-on chicken thighs or you can use deboned breasts, legs, and wings. This dish features a delicious medley of vegetables like yellow onion, garlic, mushrooms, and bell pepper that lend it a variety of flavors. To make the sauce, crushed tomatoes and tomato paste are added together with fresh herbs like rosemary, parsley, and basil for an herbaceous flavor and spicy kick from red pepper flakes and dried oregano. To prepare this easy dish, start by heating some oil in a large pan or dutch oven. Then, add the chicken to cook until it's golden brown on both sides before removing from pan. Add the onions, garlic, mushrooms and bell peppers to the same pan and sauté for a few minutes before adding in the crushed tomatoes and tomato paste. Simmer everything together until mixed well then add in your herbs and spices. Put the chicken back into the pan, cover and cook for about 30 minutes until chicken is cooked through. Serve over pasta or with a side of mashed potatoes and enjoy! With easy to find ingredients, you can make this easy and delicious Chicken Cacciatore dish in no time. Bon Appétit!

Buffalo Chicken Pizza

Ingredients
1 lb. pizza dough, divided in half.
cornmeal, for pan.
4 tbsp. butter.
1/4 c. hot sauce (such as Frank's), plus more for drizzling (optional)
1/2 tsp. garlic powder.
2 c. shredded cooked chicken.
8 oz. ball mozzarella, torn.
1/3 c. blue cheese, crumbled.

If you're looking for an easy and fast chicken recipe, try our delicious Buffalo Chicken Pizza! This easy to prepare pizza packs a punch of flavor with its combination of hot sauce, garlic powder, shredded cooked chicken, mozzarella cheese and crumbled blue cheese.

To begin making this mouth-watering pizza, preheat your oven to 400°F and lightly dust a pizza pan or baking sheet with cornmeal. Roll out one half of the pizza dough on the prepared pan and brush with melted butter. Sprinkle garlic powder over the top.

Next, combine the hot sauce with two cups of shredded cooked chicken and layer on top of the pizza dough. Place torn mozzarella cheese over the chicken and sprinkle crumbled blue cheese on top

Roll out the remaining pizza dough and place it on top of the pizza. Pinch together to seal, then brush with melted butter. Bake in preheated oven for 25-30 minutes, or until crust is golden brown.

Once done, remove from oven and let cool for a few minutes before slicing. Serve warm with extra hot sauce for drizzling, if desired. Enjoy!

This easy and delicious Buffalo Chicken Pizza is sure to be a hit with the family! Try it today and impress your loved ones with this easy-to-make dish.

Chicken Alfredo

Ingredients

1 tbsp olive oil.
4 skinless boneless chicken thighs, cut in half.
300g fettuccine, or tagliatelle.
1 tbsp butter.
200ml double cream.
½ a nutmeg, grated.
100g parmesan.
parsley, chopped, to serve.

This easy and fast chicken alfredo recipe is the perfect midweek meal. It only takes around 30 minutes to prepare and cook, so you can have a delicious dinner on the table in no time.

To make this dish, start by heating the olive oil in a large frying pan over medium-high heat. Once hot, add the chicken thighs and cook for 5 minutes on each side until golden.
Next, cook the fettuccine according to packet instructions.

Meanwhile, in a separate saucepan, melt butter over medium heat. Add cream, nutmeg and parmesan to the pan and bring to a gentle simmer. Stir occasionally for around 10 minutes until the sauce is thick and creamy.

Once your chicken and pasta are cooked, add them to the cream sauce and stir to combine.
Serve with a sprinkle of chopped parsley for extra flavour. Enjoy!

Chicken Enchilada Casserole

This easy and fast Chicken Enchilada Casserole is a great weeknight meal option. With just 5 simple ingredients - chicken, tortillas, beans, cheese and enchilada sauce - you can have this delicious dish on the table in no time.

To prepare the casserole, simply layer the chicken, tortillas, beans and cheese in a casserole dish. Top with enchilada sauce and bake until golden brown.

Serve with a side of sour cream and chopped tomatoes for a complete meal. This easy chicken recipe is sure to become one of your favorite weeknight meals! Enjoy!

Chicken Tortellini

Ingredients

2 tablespoons olive oil.
8 oz boneless skinless chicken breast, cut into 1/4-inch slices.
3 cups fresh small broccoli florets.
2 teaspoons chopped garlic.
1 1/2 cups Progresso™ chicken broth (from 32-oz carton)
2 packages (9 oz each) refrigerated cheese tortellini.
1 cup milk.

Preparing a healthy and easy dinner for the kids doesn't have to be a hassle. This delicious Chicken Tortellini is sure to please everyone at the table.

To make this dish, start by heating two tablespoons of olive oil in a large skillet over medium-high heat. Once it's hot, add the chicken slices and cook for about 4 minutes until they're no longer pink. Add the broccoli florets, garlic, and a pinch of salt, then cook for another 3 to 4 minutes.

Next, pour in the Progresso™ chicken broth and bring it to a boil over high heat. Once boiling, add the tortellini and cook for about 8 minutes until the pasta is cooked through. Then, reduce the heat to low and stir in the milk. Simmer for a few more minutes until it thickens up a bit. Taste and season with salt and pepper if needed.

Serve the tortellini with some extra grated Parmesan cheese on top. Enjoy! This Chicken Tortellini is a healthy and delicious dinner that your kids are sure to love. It's quick and easy, ready in just 30 minutes. Enjoy!

*Note: You can customize this dish with other vegetables like mushrooms, bell peppers or spinach. For added protein, you can also add shrimp or cooked sausage. Enjoy!

Enjoy! With its delicious flavor and simple preparation, this Chicken Tortellini is a surefire winner for any family dinner. It's the perfect healthy and easy dinner for kids - ready in just 30 minutes! Bon appetit!

Chicken Quesadillas

Ingredients

1 pound skinless, boneless chicken breast, diced.
1 (1.27 ounce) packet fajita seasoning.
1 tablespoon vegetable oil.
2 green bell peppers, chopped.
2 red bell peppers, chopped.
1 onion, chopped. …
10 (10 inch) flour tortillas.
1 (8 ounce) package shredded Cheddar cheese.

Chicken quesadillas make for a healthy and easy dinner for the whole family. To start preparing, dice the boneless chicken breasts and season with fajita seasoning. In a large skillet over medium heat, heat vegetable oil and add in the diced chicken breast, green bell peppers, red bell peppers, and onions. Cook until vegetables are softened and chicken is cooked through. To assemble the quesadillas, place about ¼ cup of cheese onto one side of a tortilla. Top with cooked vegetables and chicken, then add another ¼ cup of cheese to the top. Fold over into a half-moon shape and cook in a skillet on medium-high heat until golden brown. Repeat this process with the remaining tortillas. Serve warm and enjoy!

For a fun variation, try adding black beans to the quesadillas or swapping out Cheddar cheese for Monterey Jack. Using flavorful ingredients like jalapenos, salsa, and guacamole can also liven up this classic dish. Chicken quesadillas make for a healthy and delicious dinner that can be customized to fit the tastes of any family. Enjoy!

Sesame Chicken Meatballs

Ingredients

1 pound ground chicken.
½ cup breadcrumbs.
2 tablespoons soy sauce.
1 tablespoon Shaoxing wine (or mirin)
½ tablespoon sesame oil.
1 tablespoon ginger, freshly grated.
½ teaspoon garlic powder.
2 tablespoons green onions, finely chopped.

These chicken sesame meatballs are a healthy and easy dinner option that your kids will love. To prepare the meatballs, simply combine all of the ingredients in a large bowl and mix together until everything is well-incorporated. Once the mixture is ready, form it into small balls with your hands. Place them on a parchment paper-lined baking sheet, and bake at 350°F for about 20 minutes or until the meatballs are cooked through. Serve hot with a side of your favorite vegetables or salad. Enjoy!

This is an easy recipe that requires minimal preparation time, making it perfect for busy weeknights. Plus, you can use leftover meatballs as a quick and simple lunch the next day. So when you're looking for a healthy dinner option that your kids will love, give these chicken sesame meatballs a try!

Chicken Noodle Casserole

Ingredients
12 oz. wide egg noodles.
10.5-oz. cans cream of chicken soup.
1 c. whole milk.
1 c. shredded sharp cheddar cheese.
1 tsp. ground black pepper.
1/2 tsp. kosher salt.
3 c. cooked, shredded chicken (from 1 rotisserie chicken)
1/2. small yellow onion, finely chopped.

Making a chicken noodle casserole is an easy and healthy dinner option for kids. To begin, preheat your oven to 400 degrees Fahrenheit. In a large pot over medium heat, cook the egg noodles according to package directions. Drain the cooked noodles and set aside.

In a medium-sized bowl, combine the cream of chicken soup, milk, shredded cheese, ground black pepper and kosher salt. Stir until the ingredients are completely blended.

In a 9-by-13-inch baking dish, spread the cooked egg noodles. Top with the shredded chicken and onion pieces. Pour the cream of chicken mixture over the noodles and chicken, spreading evenly to ensure everything is coated.

Bake for 25 minutes until the cheese is melted and bubbly. Let cool for about 10 minutes before serving. Enjoy!

This chicken noodle casserole provides a comforting, delicious and healthy dinner option for kids. It's quick to prepare, full of flavor and sure to please everyone at the table.

Chicken Tacos

Ingredients

¼ cup olive oil.
2 medium yellow onions, finely chopped.
2 bell peppers (any color), finely chopped.
4 cloves garlic, finely chopped.
2 pounds ground chicken (not extra-lean all breast meat)
1 tablespoon paprika.
2 teaspoons ancho chili powder.
1½ teaspoons ground cumin.

Preparing chicken tacos is a healthy and easy dinner option that kids will love. To make them, begin by heating ¼ cup of olive oil in a large skillet over medium-high heat. Add in chopped onions and bell peppers, as well as the minced garlic, stirring everything until it's lightly browned and fragrant.

Then, add in the ground chicken, breaking it up with a spoon as you stir. Once the chicken is cooked through, sprinkle in paprika, ancho chili powder and cumin. Stir everything to combine and let it cook for 3-4 minutes until all of the flavors have melded together.

Once done, serve your chicken tacos with tortillas, your favorite toppings and a side dish. Enjoy!

This is an easy yet tasty way to whip up a healthy dinner for the kids!

By following these easy steps, you can have a delicious batch of chicken tacos ready in no time. Not only are they healthy and delicious, but your kids will love them too! Try it out today for a quick and tasty dinner option.

Enjoy!

Chicken Noodle Soup

Ingredients
2 tablespoons unsalted butter.
1 onion, diced.
2 carrots, peeled and diced.
2 celery ribs, diced.
3 cloves garlic, minced.
8 cups chicken stock.
2 bay leaves.
Kosher salt freshly ground black pepper, to taste.

Chicken noodle soup is a delicious, healthy and easy dinner option for kids. To prepare it, start by melting the butter over medium heat in a large pot. Add the onion, carrots and celery to the pot and cook until softened, about 5 minutes. Stir in garlic until fragrant, about 1 minute. Pour in chicken stock, bay leaves, salt and pepper. Bring the soup to a boil. Reduce heat and simmer for 15 minutes or until the vegetables are tender. Finally, add noodles and cook according to package instructions. Serve hot with your favorite toppings such as shredded cheese, croutons or chopped parsley. Enjoy!

Cornflake Chicken

Making Cornflake Chicken is a healthy and easy dinner for kids. It is simple to prepare, only requiring some milk, an egg, flour, garlic powder, salt and pepper, cornflakes and chicken breasts.

To begin preparing your meal, stir the milk, egg, flour, garlic powder, salt and pepper together in a bowl. Then take a chicken breast and dredge it in the milk mixture and roll it in the cornflakes to coat. Place on a baking sheet or dish, and bake for 45 minutes until the juices run clear and no longer pink at the bone.

Enjoy your delicious Cornflake Chicken! It's sure to be a hit with the kids!

This meal is a great option for busy evenings when time is of the essence. It's nutritious and tasty, so everyone will be looking forward to dinner. With this easy-to-follow recipe, you can make Cornflake Chicken in no time!

Happy cooking!

Chicken Fajitas

Here is a list of ingredients for chicken fajitas:
- 1 pound boneless, skinless chicken breasts or thighs, sliced into thin strips
- 2 bell peppers (any color), sliced
- 1 large onion, sliced
- 3 tablespoons lime juice
- 2 tablespoons olive oil
- 2 teaspoons chili powder
- 1 teaspoon paprika
- 1 teaspoon cumin
- 1 teaspoon garlic powder
- Salt and pepper, to taste
- 8-10 flour or corn tortillas
- Optional toppings: shredded cheese, sour cream, avocado, salsa, fresh cilantro, etc.

Instructions:
1. In a large bowl, mix together the lime juice, olive oil, chili powder, paprika, cumin, garlic powder, salt, and pepper.
2. Add the chicken, bell peppers, and onions to the bowl and toss to coat with the marinade. Let marinate for at least 30 minutes, or up to 2 hours.
3. Heat a large skillet or griddle over high heat. Add the marinated chicken and vegetables to the skillet, and cook for 5-7 minutes, until the chicken is cooked through and the vegetables are tender.
4. Warm the tortillas in the microwave or on a griddle.
5. To assemble the fajitas, place a few spoonfuls of the chicken and vegetables mixture onto a tortilla, and top with your favorite toppings. Roll up the tortilla and enjoy!

Pineapple Chicken Casserole

Here's a list of ingredients for a pineapple chicken casserole:

2 cups cubed cooked chicken
1 can (10-1/2 ounces) condensed cream of mushroom soup
1 cup pineapple tidbits
2 celery ribs, chopped
1 tablespoon chopped green onion
1 tablespoon reduced-sodium soy sauce
1 can (3 ounces) chow mein noodles, divided

Instructions:

Preheat the oven to 350°F (175°C).

In a large bowl, combine the chicken, cream of mushroom soup, pineapple tidbits, chopped celery, green onion, and soy sauce.

Pour the mixture into a 2-quart baking dish.

Crush half of the chow mein noodles and sprinkle them over the top of the chicken mixture.

Bake the casserole in the preheated oven for 30 minutes, or until heated through and the top is golden and crispy.

Serve the casserole hot, garnished with the remaining chow mein noodles and additional chopped green onion, if desired. Enjoy!

Lemon Mushroom Chicken

Ingredients:

4 chicken breasts (about 3/4 pound total)
1 1/2 tbsp unsalted butter, divided
8 oz cremini mushrooms, sliced
1/4 tsp salt
1/2 cup dry sherry
1/4 cup lemon juice
1/2 cup heavy cream
2 1/2 cups baby spinach

Instructions:

Season the chicken breasts with salt and pepper.

In a large pan, heat 1 tbsp of butter over medium heat. Add the chicken breasts and cook for about 4-5 minutes on each side, or until golden brown and fully cooked. Remove the chicken from the pan and set aside.

In the same pan, add the remaining butter and sliced mushrooms. Cook the mushrooms for about 4-5 minutes, or until they are tender and lightly browned.

Add the sherry to the pan and use a wooden spoon to scrape the bottom of the pan to release any browned bits. Cook the sherry for about 2 minutes, or until it has reduced by half.

Add the lemon juice and heavy cream to the pan and stir to combine. Cook the sauce for about 2-3 minutes, or until it has thickened slightly.

Return the chicken breasts to the pan and add the baby spinach. Stir to combine and cook for about 2 minutes, or until the spinach has wilted.

Serve the chicken with the lemon mushroom sauce on top. Enjoy!

Air Fryer Chicken Meatballs

Into a large mixing bowl, add ground chicken, egg, bread crumbs, parmesan cheese, salt, pepper, garlic powder, onion powder, paprika, olive oil and parsley and mix until combined.

No, take a heaping tablespoon from the chicken mixture and shape it into a ball.

Next, place the chicken meatballs in the air fryer basket and set to 375°F for 12-15 minutes flipping halfway through. This healthy recipe is an easy and fast way to make delicious, low budget meals! You can top these chicken meatballs over pasta or a salad for a complete meal. With air frying, you don't have to worry about the oil or the mess. No need to stand over a hot stove, just preheat and enjoy healthy eating in no time! You can also try this recipe with ground turkey or beef for even more delicious variations. Air frying has revolutionized healthy cooking; easy, fast and healthy recipes are now achievable at home without sacrificing taste. Try this easy air fryer chicken meatballs recipe and enjoy healthy eating today!

The end result: delicious, healthy air fryer chicken meatballs that are an easy and fast way to make low budget meals. With just a few ingredients and the air fryer, you can have healthy meals on the table in no time. Enjoy!

Chicken Parmigiana:

Ingredients for

2 large, skinless chicken breasts, halved through the middle
2 eggs, beaten
75g breadcrumbs
75g parmesan, grated
1 tbsp olive oil
2 garlic cloves, crushed
Half a 690ml jar of passata
1 tsp caster sugar

Instructions for preparing Chicken Parmigiana:

Preheat the oven to 200°C (400°F). Line a baking sheet with parchment paper.

Place the beaten eggs in a shallow dish and set aside. In another shallow dish, mix together the breadcrumbs and grated parmesan.

Dip each chicken breast into the beaten eggs, then coat with the breadcrumb mixture, pressing the breadcrumbs firmly onto the chicken.

Heat the olive oil in a large skillet over medium heat. Add the coated chicken breasts and cook until browned on both sides, about 3-5 minutes per side.

Transfer the chicken to the prepared baking sheet and bake in the preheated oven for 15-20 minutes, or until the chicken is cooked through and the breadcrumbs are golden brown.

While the chicken is baking, prepare the sauce. In a small saucepan, heat the garlic in the remaining olive oil until fragrant. Stir in the passata and caster sugar and cook until heated through.

Serve the chicken parmigiana topped with the warm tomato sauce, with a side of pasta or vegetables, if desired. Enjoy!

Pulled Chicken Salad

1 small roasted chicken, about 1kg
½ red cabbage, cored and finely sliced
3 carrots, coarsely grated or finely shredded
5 spring onions, finely sliced on the diagonal
2 red chillies, halved and thinly sliced
A small bunch of coriander, roughly chopped, including stalks

Instructions for preparing Pulled Chicken Salad:

Remove the meat from the roasted chicken and shred it into bite-sized pieces using two forks or your hands.

In a large bowl, mix together the shredded chicken, finely sliced red cabbage, grated carrots, finely sliced spring onions, thinly sliced red chillies, and chopped coriander.

Season the salad with salt and pepper, to taste.

To serve, arrange the salad on a large platter or divide it evenly onto individual plates. You can also drizzle some vinaigrette or your favorite dressing over the salad, if desired.

Serve the Pulled Chicken Salad immediately and enjoy!

Chicken Caesar Salad

If you want to make an easy and fast chicken caesar salad, then you've come to the right place! This recipe is easy to prepare, and uses simple ingredients that are easy to find. To start, chop 6 cups of tightly packed romaine lettuce and set aside. Next cook 1 pound of boneless skinless chicken breasts until cooked through, then cut into strips. In a bowl, mix together the chicken strips, lettuce and ½ cup of finely shredded parmesan cheese. Add in ½ cup of seasoned croutons and ¼ cup of creamy caesar dressing. Mix everything together and serve your easy and delicious chicken caesar salad! For more easy-to-make chicken recipes, check out our website for more ideas. Enjoy!

Chicken Burger

Making easy and fast chicken burgers is a great way to enjoy a tasty meal. These easy-to-prepare chicken burgers are made with only a few simple ingredients. To begin, combine the ground chicken breast, minced garlic, chopped chives, chopped oregano, lemon juice, breadcrumbs, mayo, salt and pepper in a large bowl. Mix the ingredients until they are thoroughly combined and form into patties.

Heat a skillet over medium heat and cook the chicken burgers for about 4-5 minutes on each side, or until cooked through. Serve these delicious chicken burgers with your favorite toppings such as lettuce, tomato, onion, cheese and pickles. Enjoy your easy and fast chicken burgers!

Making easy and fast chicken recipes doesn't have to be complicated when you follow this easy recipe. With just a few simple ingredients, you can enjoy delicious homemade chicken burgers that are sure to please the whole family. So don't wait - try out these easy and fast chicken burger recipes today!

Chicken Cordon Bleu Casserole

3 cups cubed cooked chicken.
4 ounces sliced deli ham, chopped.
3 cups broccoli florets.
1 cup shredded Swiss cheese.
1/4 cup dry white wine.
2 tablespoons butter, melted.
1 cup plain panko (Japanese-style bread crumbs)

Chicken Cordon Bleu Casserole is a easy and fast meal to prepare. This classic chicken recipe combines cubed cooked chicken, chopped deli ham, broccoli florets, Swiss cheese, white wine, butter and panko into one delicious dish. To make this easy and delicious casserole, preheat the oven to 375°F and spray a 9x13-inch baking dish with cooking spray. In a large bowl, combine the chicken, ham, broccoli and Swiss cheese. Pour the wine over the mixture and stir in the melted butter. Mix until all of the ingredients are well incorporated. Spread into the prepared pan and top with panko bread crumbs. Bake for 25 minutes or until the top is golden brown and the casserole is heated through. Serve with a side salad or your favorite vegetable for a complete meal. Enjoy!

Chicken Cordon Bleu Casserole is easy to make and will certainly become a family favorite. With the combination of chicken, ham, cheese and broccoli, this casserole is sure to please even the pickiest of eaters. The next time you need a fast and easy meal, give Chicken Cordon Bleu Casserole a try! Enjoy!

Crispy Chicken Tacos

Ingredients

Tortillas: corn tortillas are best.
Chicken: you can cook your own or use rotisserie chicken. ...
Smoked paprika.
Cumin.
Garlic powder.
Onion powder.
Salsa Verde: I like to use a green salsa for this recipe, but feel free to use a red salsa if you prefer.

Crispy Chicken Tacos are easy and fast to make. They can be a great addition to your chicken recipes repertoire! If you are looking for an easy way to prepare this tasty dish, look no further!

To get started, all you need is some tortillas (corn tortillas work best), cooked or rotisserie chicken, and a few easy-to-find spices such as smoked paprika, cumin, garlic powder, and onion powder.

Once you have all your ingredients ready, it's time to cook! Start by heating the tortillas on a hot skillet for about 1 minute per side. Next, mix together the chicken with the spices and salsa verde. Once everything is combined, add the chicken to the skillet and cook for about 5-7 minutes, or until the chicken is cooked through.

Finally, assemble your tacos by adding a couple spoonfuls of chicken into each tortilla and serving with your favorite toppings! Enjoy!

Chicken And Rice Casserole

Ingredients

3 chicken breasts, cut into cubes.
2 cups water.
2 cups instant white rice. ...
1 (10.75 ounce) can cream of chicken soup.
1 (10.75 ounce) can cream of celery soup.
1 (10.75 ounce) can cream of mushroom soup.
salt and ground black pepper to taste.
½ cup butter, sliced into pats.

This easy and fast chicken and rice casserole is the perfect dinner recipe for busy weeknights. It takes only minutes to prepare and can be made with minimal effort. All you need are a few easy-to-find ingredients such as chicken breasts, instant white rice, cream of chicken soup, cream of celery soup, cream of mushroom soup, salt and pepper and butter.

To begin, preheat your oven to 350°F (175°C). In a large bowl, combine the cubed chicken with all the soups, salt and pepper. Stir until everything is evenly blended. Then pour into a 9x13 inch baking dish. Next, sprinkle the instant white rice on top of the chicken mixture. Finally, dot with butter pats and cover the baking dish with aluminum foil.

Bake for about 50 minutes or until the chicken is cooked through and the rice is tender. Once done, remove from oven and let rest for 10 to 15 minutes before serving. Enjoy your easy and delicious chicken and rice casserole!

With this easy and fast chicken recipe, you can have a delicious dinner on the table in no time. Enjoy!

Buffalo Chicken Wrap

Ingredients

1 pound boneless skinless chicken breasts.
2 Tablespoons olive oil.
1/2 cup Frank's Hot Sauce.
1/2 teaspoon paprika.
1/2 teaspoon garlic powder.
pinch of salt.
4 large flour tortillas.
1/2 cup Blue cheese or Ranch dressing.

For easy and fast chicken recipes, a buffalo chicken wrap is the perfect go-to dish. It's easy to prepare and only requires a handful of simple ingredients. Start by marinating the chicken breasts in olive oil, hot sauce, paprika, garlic powder and salt for at least 30 minutes. Then heat up a skillet over medium-high heat and cook the chicken for about 10 minutes or until cooked through. Once it's cooked, chop up the chicken then warm up four large tortillas in a dry skillet. Spread equal amounts of dressing over each wrap, top off with some chopped chicken then carefully roll them up. For an extra kick of flavor, add some extra hot sauce to your wrap. Enjoy your easy and fast buffalo chicken wrap!

Peanut Butter And Jelly Wings

Ingredients
13 ounces tart cherry jelly.
1/2 cup natural creamy peanut butter.
2 tablespoons apple cider vinegar.
2 tablespoons cherry juice.
1 teaspoon sriracha.
12 chicken drumettes.
Chopped peanuts.

If you're looking for easy and fast chicken recipes, then these Peanut Butter and Jelly Wings are just what you need! With just a few simple ingredients, you can make this delicious dish in no time. To start, combine tart cherry jelly, natural creamy peanut butter, apple cider vinegar, cherry juice and sriracha in a small bowl. Use a whisk to mix everything together until smooth. Heat the mixture in a saucepan over low heat, stirring occasionally, until it begins to simmer. Once the peanut butter and jelly mixture is ready, take 12 chicken drumettes and marinate them in the mixture for 30 minutes or overnight, depending on your preference.

When you're ready to cook, preheat the oven to 375F. Place the chicken drumettes on a greased baking sheet and bake for 20-25 minutes, turning them halfway through. Once they're golden brown and cooked through, take them out of the oven and brush with more of the peanut butter and jelly mixture. Sprinkle with chopped peanuts and serve with a side of your favorite dipping sauce. Enjoy!

Lemon Chicken Orzo

Ingredients

1 tablespoon olive oil.
2 tablespoons butter.
1/2 medium onion chopped.
3 cloves garlic minced.
1/4 teaspoon Italian seasoning.
1 cup uncooked orzo pasta.
2 cups chicken broth.
2 tablespoons lemon juice.

Looking for an easy and fast chicken recipe that you can prepare in no time? The lemon chicken orzo is the perfect solution. This one-pot dish combines succulent chicken with tender orzo pasta, all spiced up with garlic and Italian seasoning. Plus, it's easy to make and ready within 30 minutes!

To start making the lemon chicken orzo, heat the olive oil and butter in a large skillet over medium-high heat. Once hot, add the chopped onion and garlic and sauté until softened and fragrant. Next, stir in the Italian seasoning before adding in the uncooked orzo pasta. Pour in the chicken broth and bring to a boil. Let the mixture simmer for about 8-10 minutes or until the orzo is cooked. Lastly, add the lemon juice and stir to combine. Enjoy your easy and tasty lemon chicken orzo!

Chicken Parmesan

Ingredients

4 skinless, boneless chicken breast halves. ...
salt and freshly ground black pepper to taste.
2 large eggs.
1 cup panko bread crumbs, or more as needed.
¾ cup grated Parmesan cheese, divided.
2 tablespoons all-purpose flour, or more if needed.
½ cup olive oil for frying, or as needed.
½ cup prepared tomato sauce.

Chicken Parmesan is an easy and fast dinner recipe that is sure to please the whole family. Preparing it at home can be a quick and easy task if you follow the right steps.

To start, season the chicken breasts with salt and pepper then dip in beaten eggs and coat with bread crumbs mixed with half of the Parmesan cheese. Heat the olive oil in a large skillet over medium-high heat, add the chicken and cook until golden brown on both sides. Transfer to a greased baking dish and top with the tomato sauce and remaining Parmesan cheese.

Bake at 350 degrees Fahrenheit for 20-25 minutes or until the chicken is cooked through. Serve with your favorite sides and enjoy!

This easy chicken Parmesan recipe is a great go-to meal that comes together in no time. Try it today and make sure to share the delicious results with friends and family. Bon appétit!

Asian Orange Chicken

Ingredients

1 ½ cups water.
⅓ cup rice vinegar.
¼ cup lemon juice.
2 ½ tablespoons soy sauce. Great Value Less Sodium Soy Sauce, 15 fl oz.
2 tablespoons orange juice.
1 cup packed brown sugar.
2 tablespoons chopped green onion.
1 tablespoon grated orange zest.

Asian Orange Chicken is an easy and fast dish to make for dinner. With its blend of sweet, tangy, and savory flavors, it'll quickly become a favorite among chicken recipes. To prepare this dish all you need is the ingredients listed above plus some cubed chicken breast.

First off, in a medium saucepan combine the water, rice vinegar, lemon juice, soy sauce, orange juice and brown sugar. Stir until the mixture starts to boil. Then reduce the heat to low and let simmer for 8-10 minutes or until the sauce has thickened slightly.

Meanwhile in a deep skillet over medium heat cook your chicken cubes until they are lightly browned and cooked through.

When the sauce is ready, add it in with the chicken and let cook for a few minutes until everything is evenly coated. Finally, garnish with green onions and orange zest for extra flavor and serve over hot white rice. Enjoy your easy to make yet tasty Asian Orange Chicken!

Baked Chicken Thighs

This easy and fast baked chicken thighs recipe is perfect for busy weeknights. The combination of seasonings gives the chicken a deep flavor, while the addition of brown sugar helps to caramelize it in the oven. It's a simple yet delicious dish that you can whip up in no time!

To make this recipe, start with preheating your oven to 375 degrees Fahrenheit. Then, mix together the Italian seasoning, brown sugar, paprika, garlic powder, onion powder, salt and pepper in a small bowl. Rub the mixture all over both sides of the chicken thighs and place them on an oiled baking pan. Bake for 30-35 minutes or until the chicken reaches an internal temperature of 165 degrees Fahrenheit.

Once finished baking, let the chicken rest for a few minutes before serving. Enjoy your easy and delicious chicken dish! You can pair it with any side you like—from roasted vegetables to creamy mashed potatoes, the possibilities are endless! So next time you're in need of easy and flavorful chicken recipes, give this easy and fast baked chicken thighs recipe a try. You won't be disappointed!

Enjoy!

Indian Curry Chicken

Learning how to prepare Murgh Kari is easy and fast! This spicy Indian chicken recipe can be prepared in less than 30 minutes. You will need some basic ingredients including garam masala, coriander, turmeric, cayenne pepper, tomato, yogurt, onion, garlic and ginger.

To begin, start by heating some oil in a large pan over medium heat. Then add the chicken pieces and let it cook until they are lightly browned. Once the chicken is ready, add the onion and garlic to the pan and let it fry for about 2 minutes.

Next, add all of your spices to the pan and mix well. Then pour in the tomato and yogurt, stirring continuously until everything is fully combined.

Finally, reduce the heat to low and let the Murgh Kari simmer for about 15 minutes before it's ready to be served. Enjoy your delicious Indian chicken curry with some steamed basmati rice or naan bread.

Murgh Kari is an easy and flavorful chicken recipe that you can make in no time. It's the perfect meal to share with your loved ones and enjoy a delicious dinner! Try out this classic Indian dish today!

You may also wish to try variations of Murgh Kari, like adding vegetables or experimenting with different spices to make it your own. We hope you enjoyed learning how to prepare Murgh Kari and that you have a wonderful time cooking up this easy and delicious Indian dish!

I want to take a moment to express my heartfelt gratitude for your recent purchase of my recipe book. As a passionate food lover, nothing makes me happier than sharing my favorite recipes with others. Your decision to invest in my book not only supports my dream, but also shows your commitment to expanding your culinary horizons.

I sincerely hope that the recipes in the book will inspire you to try new things and add some excitement to your meals.

Thank you again for your support and for being a part of this journey with me. I hope my book will bring you many happy and delicious moments in the kitchen.

www.ingramcontent.com/pod-product-compliance
Lightning Source LLC
Chambersburg PA
CBHW041150110526
44590CB00027B/4182